SITES INSIGHT

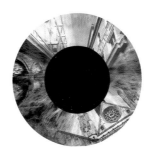

www.ahfund.org.uk

THE ARCHITECTURAL
HERITAGE FUND

First published 2006 by The Architectural Heritage Fund, Alhambra House,
27-31 Charing Cross Road, London WC2H 0AU.

Copyright © The Architectural Heritage Fund and the authors 2006.

The moral right of the authors to be identified as such has been asserted.

All opinions expressed in this book are the authors' own and do not
necessarily represent the views of the Architectural Heritage Fund.

A CIP catalogue record for this book is available from the British Library.
ISBN 0-9515468-2-1
ISBN 978-0-9515468-2-6 (from January 2007)

Pre-press Proofreading: PerfectWord, Telford
Design by Premm Design, Mortlake, London
Printed and bound in Great Britain by Chandlers Print, Bexhill-on-Sea, Sussex
Paper supplied by Southern Paper Group Ltd

Exploring the UK's buildings and landscapes through the eyes of public figures, in celebration of The Architectural Heritage Fund's 30th anniversary

Written by: Nicola Benedetti, Simon Callow, George Ferguson, Charlie George, Michael Gove, Katherine Jenkins, Griff Rhys Jones, Jude Kelly, David Lammy, Emily Maitlis, Tony Pidgley, Sean Rafferty

Edited by: Colin Amery

Assisted by: Diane Kendal, Ian Lush

CONTENTS

THIRTY YEARS ON

The British summers of 1976 and 2006 were both staggeringly hot – but that is where the resemblance ends. The mood of the times is startlingly different. Britain wasn't embroiled in international wars in 1976, "cod wars" in the North Sea and Irish troubles seem more parochial than the invasions and international terrorism of 2006. America in 1976 was politely celebrating its bicentenary and Concorde flew the Atlantic commercially for the first time. As a follow up to the 1975 European Architectural Heritage Year the British Government granted some funds to set up an Architectural Heritage Fund in 1976, as a charity to promote the conservation of historic buildings in the UK. For the last 30 years the AHF has done just that by providing advice, information and financial assistance for projects undertaken by Building Preservation Trusts and other charities throughout the UK.

This book, while marking the passing of 30 years, also celebrates our love and enthusiasm for Britain's heritage of historic buildings. The AHF had the idea to ask a wide range of people for their informal reaction to the heritage that has in some way affected their lives. The people we asked are, with a few exceptions, not involved day by day with restoring buildings – their talents are playing football, acting, singing or directing, working in the media and politics. But they all have their own particular response to places that have influenced them, which they need and are inspired by. The range is wide but with some common threads.

It is in childhood, often at school or in church, that the seeds of a response to the past are planted. Parks and landscapes feature strongly and nostalgia for the simple joys of feeding the ducks or being alone or getting lost in a beautiful place is frequently mentioned. If there is a common theme it is that nostalgia is not just for the past as itself, but for the past as something that has shaped us. This can take the form of wanting to understand and preserve national characteristics or trying to keep the patina and atmosphere of age in historic buildings. The nebulous quality of this thing we call heritage is now also something that has to be codified, listed, restored, accessed, interpreted, and above all funded. It is a very small part of any government's agenda and the great success of the AHF is that its advice and loans to Building Preservation Trusts acknowledges the local qualities they want to preserve. On the whole our Grade 1 listed buildings are looked after but it is the whole canvas that matters and the small familiar buildings and places are just as important but far more delicate.

In 1976 I was an editor on *The Architecture Review* which in its eclectic way saw the point of the whole architectural picture, writing as much about the past as the avant garde. 1976 was also the year when Big Ben stopped for several months – time stood still – which it seldom does in the world of buildings and development. But maybe it was that pause in the passage of time that provided the opportunity to clarify the practical approach to preserving the past that defines the Architectural Heritage Fund. Thirty is very young and there is a lot to do. If our work succeeds in inspiring others in the way that the past has inspired our contributors to this book we will not have worked in vain. The essays that follow speak clearly for themselves. They describe a wonderful range of feelings and emotions. Poignant sadness at what has been lost; serious determination to renew while rescuing the past; an awareness of ghosts; a dislike of history sanitised or cleaned up for theme parks; and a good dose of unashamed nostalgia. Let the authors speak and through them understand the whole point of valuing the past.

A BRIEF HISTORY OF
THE ARCHITECTURAL HERITAGE FUND

The ideas which led to the formation of The Architectural Heritage Fund (AHF) emerged in the late 1960s, in particular following a survey by the Civic Trust of the work of 21 building preservation trusts (BPTs), which showed that more historic buildings could be saved if trusts had access to working capital through low-interest loans. In 1971 this recommendation was included in a report which concluded that "a National Buildings Conservation Fund with a target of £1 million should be established" and the recommendation was subsequently accepted by the Secretary of State for the Environment, who announced that the Government would provide up to £500,000 in matching finance. By May 1976 funds and pledges had reached around £100,000 and these were matched by the Government, as part of its response to the 1975 'European Year of Architectural Heritage', enabling the newly-established Architectural Heritage Fund to announce its first call for applications.

The AHF's Council of Management met to consider the first applications in November 1976, and offered six loans, ranging from £4,000 to £27,000. For the first 20 years most of the projects supported by the AHF were undertaken by 'revolving fund' BPTs, established to acquire, repair, convert and then sell on properties, recycling any surpluses into the next project. In this way the AHF's money recycles too, with the loan repaid from the proceeds of the sale, together with a small amount of interest.

The AHF deliberately kept its criteria simple: buildings had to be listed (or in a conservation area but of significant merit), the applicant had to be a charity and the project had to involve either a change of ownership and/or a change of use for the building – meaning that the AHF would not fund maintenance, only projects where a building was being given a new life.

From the beginning, the AHF identified the need to advise local community groups on the formation of a suitable vehicle for their restoration work – usually a BPT – and with the approval of the Charity Commission the AHF publishes a standard governing document for a BPT in England and Wales, with similar documents for groups in Scotland and Northern Ireland, which have proved invaluable and saved thousands of pounds for small organisations in legal fees.

As the AHF developed, so too did the type of projects it funded. Initially mainly residential, soon the AHF was supporting charities in rescuing former industrial buildings, disused town halls and schools, farms and cottages, gothic follies and redundant churches. The 1980s were a time of boom and bust for the economy, especially the property market, and this is reflected in the AHF's activities, which grew from loans and commitments totalling under £1 million in 1980 to £5.6 million in 1990.

The most significant change of the 1990s was the formation of the Heritage Lottery Fund as one of the distributors of grants from the new National Lottery. This made unprecedented funds available for the restoration of buildings, and projects which had hitherto been considered impossible were able to be undertaken. The AHF extended the scope of its grants programme towards

options appraisals (then called feasibility studies) for any charity, and grants for project organiser and administration costs exclusively for BPTs. These grants are now supported by match funding in England and Scotland from English Heritage and Historic Scotland, and the AHF also receives support towards its overheads from those two funders and from Cadw in Wales and the Department of the Environment in Northern Ireland.

Some headline statistics show the extent of the AHF's work over the last 30 years. More than 1,000 projects have been funded, and over £90 million has been offered in loan funding. The average loan is now over £250,000, whilst as recently as 1999 it was just £120,000. Since the introduction of grants in 1990, more than £3.5 million has been offered. Alongside its grants and loans programme, the AHF has always led the way in its development work, and in particular in the advice and support it gives to community groups, to local authorities and to other key bodies through lectures, training courses and conference appearances. The AHF's profile has been raised by its well-regarded publications, including the *Annual Review*, *How to Rescue a Ruin* and its funding directory *Funds for Historic Buildings*, now in the form of an online database; it has a highly-praised website and is one of the key consultants to the BBC's *Restoration* series.

Recently the AHF has been extending its contacts with bodies outside the heritage world, has broadened its engagement with national, regional and local government and has contributed to important policy initiatives through representation on groups such as the ODPM's Community Assets Ownership Work Group. The AHF continues to hold major events to promote its main message: that locally-based, largely volunteer-run charities can lead large-scale regeneration projects by finding viable new uses for historic buildings, and that these projects are a key driver of economic well-being, sustainability and community cohesion.

Ian Lush
Chief Executive
The Architectural Heritage Fund

PREVIOUS PAGE
Rashleigh Cottages, Polmear, Cornwall
THIS PAGE
Top: Denver Mill, Denver, Norfolk
Right: St Andrew's in the Square, Glasgow

SLOUGH ESTATES

Slough Estates International plc (SEI) develops and invests in property located in the UK, Continental Europe and North America. The focus is on edge-of-town, flexible business space providing multi-use facilities for manufacturing, light industrial, research and development, logistics, warehousing and offices. The company is listed on the London Stock Exchange.

SEI purchased the 125 acre former Royal Aircraft Establishment (RAE) site at Farnborough in 1999. Subsequently Slough has master planned the site, undertaken infrastructure work and commenced development. The current phase includes construction of new office space and refurbishment of some of the existing buildings to create a modern business park environment.

The integration of the buildings in an area now referred to as the Historic Quarter forms a key part of this strategy. These retained buildings include a number of Grade 1 listed buildings, which are historically important. The buildings were used as wind tunnels predominantly for aviation research and development purposes. SEI have also undertaken work on the restoration and erection of an historic airship hangar within a large open space, which will become the new focal point of the park. The reconstruction of the structure at 70ft tall and some 250ft long is now nearing completion. The works to the Historic Quarter are due for completion in early 2007.

We are very grateful to Slough Estates, principal sponsor of the AHF's 30th Anniversary year, and to all the companies listed on these pages for their generous support.

BARCLAYS

Barclays would like to congratulate everyone associated with The Architectural Heritage Fund on reaching its 30th Anniversary. We are especially pleased to have become the new bankers to the AHF in such a momentous year.

In the AHF's 2004-05 *Annual Review*, Ian Lush, AHF's Chief Executive, stressed the importance of successful partnerships between Local Authorities and the Building Preservation Trust or Charity running the project. There is little doubt that the partnership between the AHF and its clients is also key, both in terms of providing finance and in terms of on-going support and advice to the project organisers.

Barclays Business Banking supports 750,000 UK businesses from start-ups to public quoted companies. We also strongly believe that a partnership approach to our customers is vitally important and is key to all we do. With dedicated Relationship Managers and direct-dial telephone support from our local support teams we are committed to providing a value-added service to our customers throughout the UK.

So well done AHF on your successful past and good luck for further success in the future.

For further information please contact;
Mark Gregory
Bromley Business Banking
E: mark.gregory@barclayscorporate.com
T: 07775 542265

BATES WELLS & BRAITHWAITE

Congratulations to AHF on the 30 years of providing funding to building preservation trusts and other charities working to preserve the heritage of the United Kingdom.

Bates Wells & Braithwaite have acted as solicitors to the AHF in England and Wales for several years advising on the legal documentation required to enable grants and loans to be made to fund building preservation projects. Whilst protecting the AHF's position as funder, we take a practical approach, bearing in mind the AHF's aim to have projects funded and works carried out.

We are experienced in handling all types of property transactions whether for charity and voluntary sector organisations or commercial organisations bringing a commercial approach borne out of a breadth of vision and experience.

Bates Wells & Braithwaite is a successful commercial law firm with a pre-eminent reputation in the provision of services to charities and social enterprises. This unique firm combines strong corporate, charity, employment, property, litigation and immigration practices with a general emphasis on public interest work and the arts.

For further information please contact;
Anthony Cartmell
E: a.cartmell@bateswells.co.uk
T: 020 7551 7732

CHANDLERS

Chandlers Printers were established in Bexhill-on-Sea, East Sussex in 1911.

During almost 100 years of trading we have built a strong reputation for both high quality printed work and reliability. At the end of 2005 we relocated to a new manufacturing site, again in Bexhill-on-Sea. Considerable investment took place at the time in a variety of new plant and equipment, which has further enhanced the print production facilities we can offer. With the ability to produce a whole variety of printed matter from brochures, annual reports, leaflets, periodicals and book work we never compromise on quality, whatever the product.

A considerable number of our customers are from the not-for-profit and heritage sectors and are as diverse as the Civic Trust, Crisis, the Missions to Seafarers and the T.U.C.

We are proud to have worked with the AHF for the full 30 years of their existence and we are delighted to be asked to produce and sponsor this anniversary book.

For further information please contact;
Steve Hollamby
E: sales@chandlers.co.uk
T: 01424 212 684

DRIVERS JONAS

Drivers Jonas is a multidisciplinary practice of chartered surveyors and property consultants. The firm is an independent partnership founded in 1725 now with over 500 people in the UK (London, Birmingham, Manchester, Edinburgh, Glasgow) and Europe.

We have a large and experienced Culture & Heritage sector team that brings together disciplines from across the firm. With over 70 clients including museums, galleries, performing arts venues, heritage attractions, libraries, and other public buildings, we provide services based on solid experience and an enthusiasm for the sector.

We help clients develop a vision for their property; we advise on methods for realising this vision; and we manage the delivery mechanisms needed to turn vision into reality: that is from strategic advice to project management, as well as many other technical disciplines.

We are on four Office of Government Commerce (OGC) framework contracts, so we can be engaged by public sector clients at competitive rates without further OJEU tendering. Our annual Culture & Heritage seminar has become a popular event for exploring current issues. This year we produced the well-received 'Heritage Works, the role of historic buildings in regeneration', for the RICS, British Property Federation and English Heritage.

For further information please contact;
Rob Colley
E: robcolley@driversjonas.com
T: 020 7896 8075

KINGSTON SMITH

Kingston Smith LLP is one of the UK's top 20 UK accountancy and auditing firms. With 46 partners spanning six offices across London and the South East, the firm supports entrepreneurial businesses, charities, education and religious organisations, trade, professional associations and private individuals.

The ethos of Kingston Smith LLP is to help clients succeed in their commercial and financial goals. In particular they have developed significant experience in supporting growing businesses through every stage of their development. To do so, partners formulate a deep understanding of the marketplace and environment in which each client competes.

Kingston Smith LLP is committed to providing a high quality service and was one of the first accountancy firms to receive ISO9001 accreditation. The firm employs around 400 people and has specialist expertise in the entertainment, sports, hospitality, manufacturing, medical, professional firms, property and TV/media industries. Willott Kingston Smith, based in the West End, is a market leader in the marketing services sector. Kingston Smith LLP is part of KS International, a global network of independent accountancy firms

For further information please contact;
Nicholas Brooks
E: nbrooks@kingstonsmith.co.uk
T: 020 7566 4000

PREMM DESIGN

Premm Design are a design and branding agency based in London SW14. Established in 1991, we have an exciting and varied list of clients ranging from the arts, broadcasters, the travel industry, communication companies through to charities.

We enjoy long term relationships with our clients, many of which we have worked with over the past 15 years. Working as a team we are committed to providing solutions for our clients that not only meet their marketing objectives but also provide them with an innovative design approach.

Congratulations to AHF on their 30 years of aiding and funding the restoration of our country's buildings. Ensuring that the architecture of our communities is preserved for future generations to enjoy.

Having worked with the AHF in designing their *Annual Review* for the past three years we were delighted to have been asked to design this book to celebrate their anniversary.

For further information please contact;
Martin Premm-Jones
E: martin@premmdesign.co.uk
T: 020 8878 7772

Specialist advisers to the not for profit sector

CONNECTING WITH HISTORIC BUILDINGS

DAVID LAMMY MP
MINISTER FOR CULTURE AND MP FOR TOTTENHAM

Interviewed by Colin Amery

When I went to see David Lammy it was both the hottest day of the year and his 34th birthday. It seemed like a good day to relax and look back. He has been a Minister in the Department of Culture Media and Sport since 2005. He was four when the Architectural Heritage Fund was founded and so I asked him when he first became aware of historic buildings. In a reflective mood he recalled his time as a chorister at Peterborough Cathedral when he was a pupil at the King's School in that city.

"I was ten when I went there to take part in voice trials to join the choir. It was the first time I had experienced a building of that historical and architectural magnificence. My home in Tottenham was modest and my church, St. Philip's, was beautiful but very Victorian. I remember the feeling of awe that I felt, and I sometimes go back there today just to sit and reflect – it remains deeply personal to me. I think you have to connect with historic buildings and I went on from London University to Lincoln's Inn when I was called to the Bar and remember those beautiful quadrangles. Also the Royal Courts of Justice and even at Harvard the buildings, although not very old by our standards, lent a 'sense of history'".

I wondered whether, bearing in mind his agenda as an MP for a deprived and culturally mixed urban constituency he thought that there was any relevance in historic buildings for young people today? His answer saw buildings as part of the storytelling of the nation.

"Talking of connecting to buildings, several adjectives come to mind – beauty, wonder, grandeur, hope, being uplifted. Not everyone sees and feels these things, but I think the important thing is that buildings do tell stories, they resonate in people's lives. There is a great movement now, particularly in historic houses, for the stones to come to life through the stories not just of the builders but also of the people who made and worked in the buildings.

In 2007 we will be commemorating the abolition of the slave trade and there are places where the story of this great movement will be revealed. I am impressed by the way the Heritage Lottery Fund has so sensitively joined up the heritage side with the built environment, architecture and history related to people and places. It is a national narrative of Britishness. How do you define Britishness? When I spoke at the British Museum last year, I attempted to analyse the unique strata of our history and the profound stories and narratives that make it up. I called it 'Our Island Stories', they take us on to a complex narrative and the stories are not prescriptive but symptomatic of Britain's story. The 'History Matters' campaign, which English Heritage is now running with The National Trust and other heritage bodies, is seeking to establish that we are here now because of where we have been."

Looking at the story of Britain I asked the young Minister whether he had any special heritage heroes?

PAGE 8
Peterborough Cathedral

THIS PAGE
Top: Peterborough Cathedral
Below & Facing page: Lincoln's Inn, London

OVERLEAF
The Royal Courts of Justice, London

"I spoke once about a heroine of mine, Octavia Hill, the great housing reformer and founder of The National Trust who brought public policy into the heritage debate, but I would not single out any particular individuals, although I do recognise the public involvement from the grassroots, which in this country in the heritage field is hugely impressive. As a Minister I am privileged to visit all parts of the country and my heroes are the 157,000 volunteers who are like a thread through our national life helping with preservation, conservation campaigns, charities, museums, communities and The National Trust. There are many, many unpaid people working in the heritage field whose expertise and skill ranges from academics to protesters and campaigners."

There was a reluctance to single out any particular building type that David Lammy considered to be under threat. Churches had to be a special case and the Chancellor of the Exchequer's moves to help church repairs by removing VAT was a practical step. He also felt that finding new uses for old buildings was the key to their future.

"We are in a strong place when it comes to the heritage. The Young Roots programme is an important initiative, there is pride in the national narrative, there is renewal that charges people up. The Heritage Lottery Fund is very important and I am glad that their proportion of lottery spend will remain the same in the future. Of course there is no bigger game in town than the Olympics. It is a great honour for Great Britain and will be a showcase for the world in London 2012. It will show our tremendous strengths and abilities to bring together past, present and future.

"When it comes to multi-culturalism, what is new about that? We are constantly telling stories and Great Britain has for a long time shown leadership under the umbrella of the Commonwealth of tolerance and multi-ethnic understanding. My parents and family came to London to work in the NHS and London Underground, and my son is very aware that he represents two heritages. He is able to see British and Commonwealth history side by side. All countries have good and bad in their history, but Britain has a huge role to encourage multi-ethnic tolerance. Despite problems like 7/7, I think people in this country rub along well together.

"I think you have to connect with historic buildings and I went on from London University to Lincoln's Inn when I was called to the Bar and remember those beautiful quadrangles."

"I just hope that we get closer in terms of tolerance and understanding. A good friend of mine, James, was killed in an awful way by the bombings of 7/7. We had studied history together from 13th century up to World War II, and it is a history of Britain fighting Fascism and extremism, and we have always had to make sacrifices to achieve tolerance. Next year's commemoration of the abolition of slavery will show those global fights led to movements like the suffragettes, Labour movement, trade unions and, coming up to date, the movement 'Make Poverty History'. These are collective and inclusive movements, and I feel our job is to make Britain the best country in the world to live. We have a huge contribution to make. We have a long history of relationships with other countries, especially the Commonwealth and the Middle East, and Britain can make a huge contribution to many communities."

The next day after our talk the House of Commons Select Committee on Culture, Media and Sport was to make its report, *Protecting and Preserving our Heritage*, when the DCMS was criticised for not arguing the case for heritage effectively enough within Government and for failing to fund the work of English Heritage adequately. I asked the Minister if he anticipated these concerns about funding and advocacy of the heritage cause.

"Although money is important and there has been a huge growth in funds across the board, other things influence heritage like education and learning. The DFES 'Laying Foundations' programme is doing well at improving the learning resources in schools to teach people about the built environment. A programme called 'Engaging Places' is working with young people in the inner cities to encourage their interest in the built environment. English Heritage has been examining itself to see if it is 'fit for purpose' and that its programmes are working in terms of heritage protection. I hope there will be a full debate on the White Paper which can improve the protection system for historic buildings so that it is more democratic, that people feel they own the built environment and that the bureaucracy is not about stopping people doing things but empowering them towards conservation. I want a 'can do' system of protection and the new National Registry will help a great deal in this task, particularly in schools.

"In the last year or so I have particularly enjoyed the heritage part of my portfolio which has been a highlight for me and an unusual one for a Culture Minister. I am hugely committed to enhancing a sense of place and purpose. History resonates in my own life. I am touched by it. I am particularly moved by my dealings with war veterans of World War I and II. When we are commemorating the last veterans of World War I and II we should not just be doing it on November 11, not just through war memorials, but through the stories of how people lived. We will find the experience of veterans through all history a humbling experience in the future. I hope we will always commemorate it with a real sense of national action."

Thank you Minister and have a Happy Birthday.

RESCUE AND REGENERATION

BY GRIFF RHYS JONES

COMEDIAN AND PRESENTER OF BBC'S *RESTORATION* SERIES

I first got really interested in the restoration of historic buildings buying old houses to live in and doing them up. My daughter, now 18, in a moment of candour once said to me "why have we never ever lived in a house that is finished?"

But I got involved in public historic buildings when I was asked to help with the Hackney Empire and that threw me into the debate about the context of our historic fabric and the struggle to save it. I have nothing but gratitude and admiration for the Heritage Lottery Fund. What could we do without it? It has poured millions into the grand old buildings of this country. At one point it seemed that it was only a matter of time for all organisations. They simply had to wait and their turn for money would come. But having been involved in the funding process myself, and having met a lot of small groups and individuals, I know that the actual process is very hard work and can leave a lot of small groups bemused and wounded. It is very hard for amateurs to face up to the complexities of the system. So it should be, perhaps, but the application forms and then the renovation itself are an exhausting process. Small volunteer groups are not experienced property developers and have to learn as they go. Unlike some big applicants, they do not have the resources to employ bureaucracies to match the Lottery. Some might better understand that the applicants in these circumstances are doing it for love. They are giving of their time, and donors are giving of their money – their own money. I was once at a British Museum party and was astonished by the opinions of a couple of off-duty officers. They were talking about a major donor I knew. They seemed to think that he had a duty to pass over his money and a duty to find even more when trouble came along. I was amazed. He could have bought a Monet or a villa in France with the money he had given, but he had chosen to help a public building instead. He had no further obligation except perhaps to wait for grateful accolades. Lottery officers, on the other hand, are performing a job on behalf of the public and part of that job is to dispense the resources fairly, evenly and helpfully. They should be aware that for every million they dispense they are asking for £200,000 to come from other sources and other pockets, sometimes private ones. This is a big ask and very, very difficult to find. The more they dispense, the more is needed.

With the Hackney Empire we went back through the whole long winded application process twice. One of the reasons given for turning us down the first time was apparently that Hackney "would find it difficult to raise the matching funding". They were right, of course. Hackney is after all one of the poorest boroughs in Europe. So the task was particularly and obviously onerous, compared with, say, Chelsea. But you cannot penalise the poor and only reward institutions which are already rich enough to have a big, paid fund-raising organisation. I can be honest. We didn't know what we were about at all. In the end, we were praised by the Arts Council for an exemplary campaign. We were told that we were the only theatre that had started building with all the money in place. I laughed. That was actually only because we didn't know otherwise. But now, having been the victim of atrocious management by the builders (amateurs that we were) we are back where we started and I still have to raise the last £700,000. No further help will be forthcoming. I have been assured.

So the Heritage Lottery Fund has complicated ways of allocating money, but what is more worrying is that it is vulnerable to political football. It must be completely independent. The government must not be able to divert funds at will, Olympic ambitions or not. It has to be kept at arm's length. Thank goodness that it has recently been granted a lease of independence. We have to fight for that to be a permanent part of its constitution. I also wish the Heritage Lottery Fund would use the enormous buying power it has in the construction industry to make building restoration and conservation more efficient. As a powerful construction body it could shoulder the burden of dealing with building delays, bankrupt contractors and difficult lawyers. It is a very big commissioner indeed. Could it be stronger willed? Now this is where government could help, by freeing up some of its resources to make it more efficient.

"I would like to see more money used to preserve coherent regions of towns and cities."

PAGE 14
Hackney Empire, London

THIS PAGE
Hackney Empire

OPPOSITE PAGE
Victoria Baths, Manchester

OVERLEAF
Interior, Hackney Empire

I have a big wish list. There is no single key to the successful regeneration of historic buildings, but I would like to see more money used to preserve coherent regions of towns and cities, more help for conservation areas and more awareness of heritage neighbourhoods. The country is still full of run down areas but some of the poorer centres of our cities might benefit more from careful preservation as opposed to wholesale rebuilding. Too often the solution has been seen as monster road access, vast buildings and huge windswept plains of concrete paving. I would also like to see more help given to the conservation building trade itself. What is wrong with slower building techniques, so that skills can be learnt and building craftsmanship maintained? This government's education policy has down-graded craft. It is easier to get a degree in tourism or media studies than to learn a much-needed, useful skill like plumbing or carpentry. Why do we need more Polish carpenters? Because there are so few trained craftsmen in all parts of this country, following the decline of technical education. When a practical building course is announced, dozens of people queue up for it. If we could educate better builders we would really be engaged in transformation of the country.

Meanwhile, I have every sympathy with what Simon Thurley and Neil Cossons are doing at English Heritage, but I worry that they are permanently engaged in a sort of philosophical conflict with their government masters. Should they be part of the government machinery at all? Perhaps, though, it is preferable that they are on the inside working for change, given how much confrontation there is already in the heritage world. Extreme attitudes are taken up and feet dug in. Goodness knows, I have plenty of intransigence myself, but those who are broadly concerned about the historical beauty of this country, and there are millions of us, have no central banner to gather under. No easy tune to march to. Plenty of politicians are privately "concerned", some care deeply but few believe there are votes in it. They may be right, when opinion can range so widely and the heritage lobby can argue so vehemently amongst itself and be so fixed about basic principles. The Green lobby has sent out an inarguable message – "support us or die". It has brought them huge success. Heritage has less urgency, rightly, but sometimes I despair that without panic nothing gets done and with a panic too much is done and most of the panics are for rebuilding.

I was recently in Monreale in Sicily, vsiting that glorious cathedral, and what you see there is largely and miraculously what was built. This semi-Byzantine wonder has been protected for centuries by autodidacts, the archbishops. Uninfluenced by fashion or the whims of government, they have endeavoured to keep the place pretty much exactly as it was when it was built, because they recognise the excellence of the original conception. Some of the values that the government promote, like accessibility, cultural diversity, and so forth are valuable but untested conceptions. I believe that it is important that conservation should be about the virtues of the building and the quality of the building first, and that should not be overwhelmed by our century's concerns however vital and urgent they seem to us today.

But thinking of churches brings me to the sad truth that society is changing and buildings must sometimes change with it. As people, we gather together less. This has meant that churches, chapels, even cinemas are not the places of assembly that they used to be. Working on *Restoration* I encounter this all over Britain. Some of our most neglected buildings are ones that people once used en masse. They were built to impress the many, so they are often also some of our most wonderful constructions. Use and change of use are crucial to regeneration. We need more help to find a future for these places. We need an independent institution to provide guidance. But institutions like English Heritage, SPAB, and the Heritage Lottery Fund are not the bodies that own the buildings. Local authorities and institutions who often do, could help define new uses for old buildings. For example, the Restoration programme drew attention to the need to restore the Victoria Baths in Manchester. The Baths are owned by the City of Manchester itself, it is surely the corporation itself that should be thinking about how to recycle historic buildings with new uses or adaptable uses. I bet they have put up a lot of new buildings, while they let that marvel rot.

And finally, we certainly need to look at our housing in all its complexity and diversity and be wary of John Prescott's simplistic views of society. But we have to recognise that some land does need to be made available. The question is how do we do this sensibly and with lasting benefits? The CPRE will have to be little less Luddite about future building on green land. Of course we need to make better use of our new cities and recycle brownfields. We need to live as densely as possible in the centres, but we have a relatively high proportion of countryside in Britain and we should not be afraid to release more land. The challenge is to build worthwhile houses of our own generation which we can be proud to leave to the next.

We should not be afraid of ideals or aesthetics. Harlow New Town was built for a new society, on strong moral principles, but looked at coldly today, it was built without enough variety. It was built without aspiration. Successful people move out of Harlow. It doesn't have space for "the crooked timber of humanity" by which I mean the individuality of people. There are after all many gradations of rich and poor in our society. There have been for millennia. I can't help feeling there always will be. I want them all to be accommodated and if possible integrated. I dislike rich ghettos as much as I dislike poor ghettos. The quality of life depends on recognising variety and accepting the nature of society as it is. All those property programmes and newspaper supplements reflect a national obsession with improvement. You cannot legislate for some non-existent, egalitarian, ticky-tacky, utopia when everyone in the country is aspiring to improve their homes to make them better or more individual. You have to accommodate that, and build in choice and variety. After all it is that evolved rich mix that makes some parts of the country so pleasing, and the absence of it that makes parts of our nation dark and terrifying. Not too much zoning, please.

I apologise if this is a bit of a rant.

LONDON'S SOUTH BANK

BY JUDE KELLY
ARTISTIC DIRECTOR, SOUTH BANK CENTRE

To be truly inspiring I believe a building must be able to provide a habitat for new life and culture, rather than purely reflect a bygone era. The South Bank Centre is such a place.

Even during this time of renovation, the SBC site is not just an empty space. The site has an identity that comes from the ideals and values with which it was created, and from the way it has changed over time. This identity is a kind of genetic imprint, an imprint that survives and shifts as external pressures act on it. In order to keep the site alive we must adhere to that imprint, taking it forwards by remembering and recovering the values that have animated the site. The way to do this is by revisiting the important history of the world festival site. In the words of War Artists who influenced the thinking that led to the Festival of Britain in 1951, the site was a place dedicated to the "propaganda of the imagination". This phrase is important to the development of the South Bank Centre because in moving forward, we need to be clear about what we are building from.

The South Bank Centre was created out of passion, out of what really constituted a revolution in which, during the war, the class structure broke open, and the gender imbalance shifted, and then after the war, those who returned created the welfare state. When Herbert Morrison described the Festival of Britain as "a tonic for the nation" he explicitly connected it to the NHS, which would look after the nation's physical health, while the Festival took seriously the idea that we all have aesthetic needs.

The Festival's makers had interrogated the word "festival". They were using the word in its ancient sense of a ritual that celebrated peace and joy but also commemorated war and death. The Festival was about more than just gaiety – it also contained within it the memory of those who had not come back from war.

The Festival was also about the power of art. During the war, artists had talked about the propaganda of the imagination – they believed that darkness could be driven out by light, and that imagination could change people's sense of what their landscape could be. When they came to work on the Festival, they were seeking to create a landscape of the imagination, a place that would inspire people to go on creative journeys of their own. They filled the site with colours, which on one level was intended to be joyous and bright after the grey drabness of the war years, but the colours were chosen with great care, the choices based on the colour theory of the modernists, the belief that as Kandinsky, the Bauhaus's preeminent colour theorist put it, "colour directly influences the soul" and that colours, both individual and in harmony, could make people look at the world in a different way.

When it came to the architecture of the site, the Bauhaus philosophy of "form follows function" was the guiding inspiration. The Festival's commissioning architect Hugh Casson recruited a team of (then) startlingly young architects to design not just the hall but the entire site. The site would be more than a few buildings

> "...visitors could walk around, listening to music... and experiencing the landscape of river, land and sky as a canvas on which the Festival's makers painted extraordinary new shapes."

in a landscaped space; Casson intended it to be "a pattern book for our new urban landscapes". Just as in the New Towns, everything within the 27 acres was designed specifically for what it was trying to do, from the curving Antelope chairs to The Royal Festival Hall with its clean lines, natural wood, space and grace, white ceilings that reflected the Thames, big windows that showed off the vistas, and the open doors that people could come through whether or not they were going into the auditorium. Even the cafés were designed down to the finest details. Misha Black's Regatta Restaurant included murals by Ben Nicholson and what Black called "a novel system of decorative pattern...derived from the diagrams made when scientists map the arrangements of atoms in crystals studied by X-ray methods" – a precursor, by almost half a century, to Damien Hirst's blend of science, art and food in Pharmacy.

The site was designed to be car-free, so that visitors could walk around, listening to music, played live or from public loudspeakers, and experiencing the landscape of river, land and sky as a canvas on which the Festival's makers painted extraordinary new shapes (the Dome of Discovery, the Skylon). They also played with the space, sending balloonists off from the site, or stretching a tight-rope across the river for Charles Elleano to cross.

The Skylon, the site's great symbol, was as brave a statement in 1951 as the Angel of the North was in 1998. In its shining and bold construction, rising into the air without visible means of support, it illustrated the idea that you can't tie art down to delivering practical and logical outcomes; art must involve a levity of the spirit. The Skylon sat among 30 sculptures and 50 murals, all part of a commitment to making a landscape that visitors could walk around and expect to be surprised and delighted. It was an exuberant site, a destination site that people came to on a day out.

The Festival was not just urban – it also honoured rural life. There were sheep and a herd of Jersey cows on display, and an emphasis on greenery and horticulture. Reviving these ideas could be the inspiration for a new generation of artists who are engaging with themes of ecology and sustainability. The Festival of Britain's commitment to science, technology and discovery was also inspirational. The Dome of Discovery featured an "escalator to outer space" leading to a planetarium, a polar theatre, and a life-sized reproduction of Captain Cook's *Endeavour*. All of this work is a precursor to the kind of work – and thinking – that should form the basis for the South Bank Centre today.

The Festival was "of Britain" but its makers had thought about what that meant. Although it marked the 100th anniversary of the Great Exhibition, and the Punch and Judy shows, pavilions and fireworks were inspired by Victorian notions of how to have a good time, Gerald Barry was determined that the Festival would not become a mindless exercise in nostalgia, announcing that there would be "no Hall of Woollens, or Pavilion of Sweetmeats or Garden of Horticulture; there would be no mammoth mounds of apples or effigies of Royalty in edible fats." (This last referred to a Prince of Wales moulded in butter at the 1924 British Empire Exhibition at Wembley). The most striking statement the Festival made was in the artists who made it happen. Many of them were refugees who had come to Britain and immediately become part of the bloodstream of Britain's creativity. Others, such as Abram Games who designed the Festival's official symbol, the angular image of Britannia decorated in bunting, were second-generation refugees who were making their own mind up about how to be British. The Festival made other statements about what constituted Britishness – for example, the Trinidad All Steel Percussion Orchestra played at the Festival, marking the first time that steelpan music was played in Britain. This philosophy of inclusiveness was the Festival's elegant and eloquent answer to the question of whether excellence and access are in conflict, and whether one needs to take priority over the other.

The Festival was always intended to end in September 1951, but its hasty dismantling after the new Conservative government came in a month later undoubtedly demonstrated a distaste for the ideals of the Festival. Only a belief that art and celebration were frivolous and unnecessary can really explain the speed and carelessness with which the site was cleared, with the Dome of Discovery sold for scrap, other treasures auctioned off, and much of the site left all but derelict.

This moment marked the beginning of a gradual period of forgetting the ideals of the Festival. The Royal Festival Hall continued to programme bold and interesting work but inevitably the emptiness of the site exerted a negative pull on the hall

PAGE 20
Royal Festival Hall, 1950s

OPPOSITE PAGE
The Skylon, Festival of Britain

THIS PAGE
Top: Festival of Britain site, 1951
Below: Interior, Royal Festival Hall

In the 1960s a new phase began for the site. The renewed excitement about it led to the opening up of the Royal Festival Hall and, in 1967-1968, the opening of the Queen Elizabeth Hall, the Purcell Room and the Hayward Gallery, and a massive expansion of the site's ability to host work, if not to produce it. Yet even at their inception, there was a disconnection between the Royal Festival Hall, contextless and becoming complacent in its fearsome reputation, and the new buildings, created by a young team of architects and inspired by very different ideals from those which had created the Festival. The development inevitably meant that the site became about buildings, devaluing the spaces in between, and that the issue became what to put into the buildings, rather than how to look at the site as a whole.

The over-and under-passes, and the overwhelming concrete, made up what was becoming a very forbidding site, difficult to navigate, colourless and badly lit. Despite this, a sense of public ownership endured. Between 1951 and 2005, of the 60 million people who came into the Royal Festival Hall, only 30 million bought tickets – people clearly continued to regard the site as their space. When the GLC started thinking more about access and equality, they built on this with the outdoor events and the open foyers policy, which was instituted in 1983. The 1980s also saw the arrival of the skateboarders, who saw the value in a dead space and made it their own. However, when it came to curating the site, an unfortunate divide had opened up between the idea of "high art" as opposed to art that was human, warm and accessible.

This division, alongside the other divisions (most crucially, the division between the Royal Festival Hall and the "cinderella spaces" of the Queen Elizabeth Hall and the Purcell Room; and the division between the Hayward as a citadel of visual arts separate from the rest of the space) were partly a result of a site developed over time, but also, arguably, to do with the original ideals having been forgotten. The site was never intended to be divided; it was conceived of as a linked space, a "woven" space, in which everything connected to everything else.

The many masterplans put forward for the site attest to the passion people still feel for it as much as to a sense that change was desperately needed to make it work. Despite the many problems with the site, it has never stopped inspiring passion and attracting creativity. This has much to do with the way it was conceived, as a creative space, an inspiring space, a thinking space, and a magnet for visionaries who dreamed their ideas into it.

Exploring our roots has raised the need for us to reconnect with some of those inspiring ideas, and also build towards an archaeology of the future. Not only has history revealed the choices made by the Festival's makers, but also about the values that were inherent in those choices. In 50 years' time, someone may excavate what we are doing, and what values seem to lie behind our choices, so we need to think really hard about them, and to make choices firm in the knowledge that we are custodians of the future.

Courtesy of the South Bank Centre Archive Royal Festival Hall, 1950s (Page 20). South Bank Centre Today Victor Rose (right)

SCOTLAND'S HERITAGE

BY NICOLA BENEDETTI
VIOLINIST, FORMER BBC YOUNG
MUSICIAN OF THE YEAR

Scotland's heritage is with me wherever I go...

As a musician, I spend much of my time travelling and staying in hotels, often with many hours to kill on my own before and after rehearsals and concerts. One of the things that sustains me through these sometimes lonely times on trains, planes or in hotel rooms is thinking about special places in Scotland, my birthplace and the country I still feel is my true home.

Among these special places is an area of south Ayrshire where my mother and her family grew up, and which I visited frequently as a child with my parents, my mother's brother and my sister. This is the Auchinleck Estate and its surrounding countryside, where my grandmother used to stay in the Gatehouse (at that time a privately-owned smallholding) and where my uncle would take us on long walks, for six hours or more, so that we felt completely lost in the trees and the glens. My uncle was very interested in the

history of the Estate and would tell us great stories about the main house, where Boswell had lived during his time as owner of the Estate and where he entertained Dr Johnson and others, and we would go to see the ruined castle with its ivy-covered walls. [The Architectural Heritage Fund supported the restoration of Auchinleck House by the Scottish Historic Buildings Trust]. The whole area was a magical place, with old caves which as a child seemed very dangerous and exciting to get to, and it is one of the parts of Scotland I miss most when I am abroad.

The whole Scottish identity is very important to me, by which I mean not just that I am Scottish, but what Scotland means to me and to so many other people – its landscapes, the vast and totally unspoilt natural spaces, and the people who are so down to earth and warm, with an easy sense of humour. I like the fact that you always know where you stand with Scottish people, there is such a refreshing honesty and natural communication – and

of course a melodious accent. Above all I always think of Scotland as a place of space and air and a special quality of light, and that is what I come back to when I am stuck in an antiseptic hotel room and I need to feel a sense of openness.

My identity though also contains my father's Italian ancestry – he was born in Italy and came to Scotland at the age of 11. I do feel a bond and affiliation to Italy, and visit often, but really want to learn to speak Italian, which will make a big difference to my ability to relate to people there properly.

One of the most positive aspects of travelling as a violinist is the opportunity to perform in some of the world's great concert venues. Recently I have been fortunate enough to play at Carnegie Hall in New York and at the Gewandhaus in Leipzig. When performing somewhere with such a rich history (the Gewandhaus is a new hall but closely associated still with Mendelssohn and with its great

"The whole Scottish identity is very important to me...its landscapes, the vast and totally unspoilt natural spaces"

orchestra) you have to try to find a balance between being intimidated and inspired. All performers are affected by the surroundings and by the atmosphere of a building, and I think this is particularly true for musicians, who are so reliant on the acoustics of a space. When it works, it can raise your performance to new heights, and some halls do seem to work really quickly, providing a perfect atmosphere in which to make music, enabling you to concentrate on playing and not be distracted by anything. At other venues it is harder and sometimes you can struggle to gain enough confidence to give your best. And of course venues change with an audience – recently I played in Verbier in Switzerland in a lovely old church, and during the rehearsal the acoustic was very resonant, too much so in fact. The organisers reassured me that it would be fine and of course they were right, with the audience in place in the evening the hall felt perfect and all my worries proved groundless.

Scotland has some wonderful concert halls, and each of them means so much to me, having performed in them at various points in the last few years. Edinburgh and Glasgow have well-known venues, of course, and I was very lucky to be asked to perform at the opening of the Scottish Parliament at Holyrood in October 2004, but there are also special halls in smaller towns and cities, such as Dundee, Aberdeen, Inverness and Perth. The Scottish audiences are always so welcoming and knowledgeable and it is always a pleasure to return home to perform in front of my own people.

A part of Scotland I have come to know most recently is Aviemore in the Cairngorns, which I have just visited for the first time. I think this is somewhere which everyone should visit, it is unique and truly spectacular. I was only able to spend a day there, but it was so peaceful, so natural and green that my batteries were completely replenished in that short time.

But every visit I make to Scotland re-charges me through its built and natural heritage, its history and its people, and I feel very lucky to be able to take this identity with me on my travels.

PREVIOUS PAGE
Scottish landscape
THIS PAGE
Right: Auchinleck Estate
OVERLEAF
Scottish landscape

SITES INSIGHT

HIGHBURY – PAST, PRESENT AND FUTURE

BY CHARLIE GEORGE
EX-ARSENAL FOOTBALLER

I first went to Highbury when I was five, with my brother-in-law. I remember being impressed with the size of the ground and the number of people, especially where we were standing on the old South Bank. The ground was very different then, with terracing at both ends, including the huge North Bank, stretching right into the corners and creating a very intense atmosphere when it was full; the main stands though were exactly as we see them now, and they made a strong impact on me as a small boy.

In those days fans used to have their favourite spots on the terraces and returned there week in, week out throughout the season. You got to know the fans around you, like one big family – so much so that if someone wasn't there one match, everyone around would ask where they'd been the following game. I vividly remember the surge in the crowd when Arsenal scored – you could end up being carried forward yards from where you had been standing. I was lucky when I was small as the men in front would pick me up and pass me over their heads until I was right at the bottom of the terrace and could walk back to where I had been standing.

It was, of course, a dream come true for a local Islington boy and Arsenal fan when I first started training with the club, and even more so when I signed as an apprentice in 1966. I'd been training with Arsenal with a lot of other lads since the age of 11, but I went on standing on the terraces with my friends in the meantime.

When I did eventually make it inside, the main (East) stand seemed magnificent – the famous entrance hall with its marble floors, and the bust of one of Arsenal's greatest managers, Herbert Chapman, and the dressing rooms were also very grand, far better than all the away grounds we went to, and way ahead of their time, even though they had been built in the 1930s. When I started as an apprentice, of course, we weren't allowed to use the first team dressing rooms, instead we changed outside in a corridor. The pitch was small, the narrowest in the league, and in my day towards the end of the season the goalmouths were largely mud and sand; recently, the Highbury pitch has been one of the best in the League, but the extra width at the new ground will suit the team's game.

For me as a local lad, running out at Highbury was amazing, especially playing for the team I had supported all my life in front of all my friends, who were cheering me on from the terraces. In those days we could have 15,000 to 20,000 fans standing on the North Bank, and when they are all chanting your name it is a fantastic feeling, the biggest thrill you will ever get in your life.

One of my favourite memories of playing at Highbury is an early one, the Final of the Fairs Cup (which is now the UEFA Cup) in 1970. In those days, the Final was still held over two legs, home and away, and we were home for the second leg, an evening match in April. It is difficult to imagine now, but in those days Arsenal

PAGE 32
Arsenal Stadium, Highbury

THIS PAGE
Below: The East Stand, exterior
Above: East Stand

OVERLEAF
Computer realisation of the
'Highbury Square' development,
viewed from the South

PAGE 36
Highbury Square

were not the successful team that they are today – we hadn't won
anything for 17 years – so I had never seen my team, the team
I loved, pick up a trophy and the pressure on us players was
enormous. We were against the top Belgian side Anderlecht
in the Final, and we had lost 3-1 in the first leg, but we turned
it around in the home game and won 4-3 on aggregate (3-0 on
the night) and I was fortunate enough to set up the winning goal.
You could say that that victory started the successful modern
era for Arsenal, because the following season we became only
the second club in the 20th century (after our deadly rivals,
Tottenham) to win the league and cup double.

I scored the winner in the FA Cup final that year at Wembley,
and that's another ground which I remember fondly. As a player,
the ground and its atmosphere does make a difference
– it is always easier playing in front of your own fans, even though
the expectation is higher, and the atmosphere at Highbury was
fantastic – it is a small ground by modern standards (when
it became all-seater it held just 38,000) but the support of the
fans was very intense. Results at all levels of football show the
advantage of playing at home, and the importance of your
familiar surroundings.

Another place I enjoyed playing was the Baseball Ground,
Derby County's old ground – I played for Derby after I left Arsenal.
At first I couldn't believe how shabby and old fashioned it seemed
after Highbury, but it had a special atmosphere and I felt very
at home there, despite the primitive facilities. I also liked Manchester
City's former home, Maine Road. But Highbury remained my first love,

and after I stopped playing I was very pleased eventually to end up back working for Arsenal as a match-day host and tour guide around Highbury, showing fans and visitors some of the behind the scenes areas as well as the marvellous main stands.

Now, like Derby, Man City and many other clubs, Arsenal are moving on, into the brand new Emirates Stadium for the start of the 2006-7 season. The reasons are economic – with a capacity of less than 40,000, compared to Manchester United's 70,000 plus, it was becoming impossible for Arsenal to compete financially and to be able to afford to bid for the best players. The new stadium will hold more than 60,000 fans and already all the seats have been sold for the first season.

People ask me if I think the game has changed too much, and they are always talking about the lack of English players in the Arsenal team. But I think the foreign players have learned from the English game as well as having brought so much to our football; the new players soon learn about the importance of the local derbies, and they are all struck by the passion and loyalty of the English fans. Football may have changed but you still have some of the same diehard supporters, following their team through thick and thin.

I am pleased, of course, that Highbury will remain, although in a new form, with the two main stands, one of which is listed, being turned into apartments, and the pitch into a series of gardens, including a memorial area for all those fans whose ashes have been scattered on the pitch. With the new stadium being less than 500 yards from Highbury, I am sure many fans will continue to walk past their old haunts as they make their way to their new seats. It is funny to think of people using the marble entrance hall to make their way to their flats, but I am sure many of the new occupants will be Arsenal fans thrilled to have the chance to live where they used to go and watch their favourite team. We can't afford to be nostalgic in the modern game, and even though Highbury has served Arsenal so well and for so long, it is time to leave.

"For me as a local lad, running out at Highbury was amazing, especially playing for the team I had supported all my life..."

A SOUTH WALES **CHILDHOOD**

BY KATHERINE JENKINS
SINGER

I was born and brought up in Neath in South Wales, and the town and its surrounding area are my own heritage, part of what has made me the person I am today. There are two very special places in Neath which mean so much to me, and which in their different ways were such an important part of my childhood.

The first is the gardens now known as The Gnoll Country Park. These are the grounds of an old stately home, which were beautifully landscaped and have now been restored as a public park and leisure area for the people of Neath. I grew up with this on my doorstep, just a couple of streets away and no more than a 10-minute walk to the entrance. From there you could walk up a hill towards the main gardens, which included some large ponds, where I would feed the ducks on stale bread, and then the ruins of the old house. These seemed very exciting and rather eerie to me as a child, but the Council then made them safe and also restored the ruins to an extent so that you could look around and see how the house was originally laid out. I was very aware of its great age and history, and it seemed a very special place. At the same time they restored the wonderful cascade and the fountains, and I have great memories of playing there with my cousins and friends. Throughout my childhood The Gnoll was a meeting point, where we would go on our bikes and get together to have fun and adventures in the huge park and playgrounds.

It was really only after I had left Neath to live in London and when I came back to visit that I realised how fortunate I had been to grow up near somewhere so remarkable, with such a great atmosphere and in such a lovely setting. When I go back now I always go up to The Gnoll and always bump into people I know. Recently when I was visiting Neath we went up to The Gnoll, there was a vintage car rally being held there, with hundreds of people around enjoying the cars and the beautiful setting.

The other place in Neath which is a huge part of my life is St David's Church. This is a huge Victorian church right in the centre of the town, and it is the largest church in Neath – and one of the biggest buildings. Its clocktower is a real landmark, which can been seen throughout the town. You could see the clocktower from the kitchen and bedroom windows of the house where I was brought up, and the Church was a huge part of my family life. My Mum teaches at the Sunday School there, and I learnt to sing there in the choir, which I was a member of for many years. It is a really important building for the community too, with lots of events happening there every week. It has sad memories for me as well, because it was where my Dad's funeral took place (he died when I was 15) and he is buried in the churchyard, but I also know that if I do eventually get married, it will be in St David's Church.

Whenever I can I try to sing there and have done a number of charity concerts, and it has a wonderful atmosphere for me as the concerts are always filled with family and friends, the people I was brought up with who have been so supportive of my career.

I was lucky in Neath, we had so many things: church choirs, amateur operatics, the national youth choir, school choirs, and I honestly don't think I would be here without that support. And I have also been really lucky already to have sung in some of the great concert halls of the world. Sydney Opera House for me was a dream come true, it was amazing to sing in such an incredible building with its fabulous setting, and to know about its history, seeing the posters of the great artists who have performed there. I have also loved singing at the Royal Albert Hall, which works really well for the voice if you choose the style of music carefully. Even though it is such a large space again I found it really inspiring to perform in such an historic and important setting.

"I return home to Wales as often as I can, and as well as going to Neath I try to visit the lovely coastline of the Gower peninsula. I may live in London now, but home to me will always mean Wales, and Neath in particular."

PAGE 38
St David's Church, Neath

THIS PAGE
Far left: Worms Head, Gower
Top right: St David's Church, Neath
Bottom right: Gnoll Country Park

OVERLEAF
The Gnoll Country Park

In a very different way I also really enjoy performing the big summer concerts outdoors, which are often in the grounds of stately homes or other historic buildings. Recently I sang at Temple Newsam in Leeds, a beautiful setting for a concert and there were 40,000 people there, and another memorable occasion was singing in the grounds of Hampton Court Palace. The audience for these concerts is different from those in conventional concert halls, they are very relaxed and often have brought picnics, and there are whole families enjoying the occasion, and I love singing in front of such a happy crowd.

The biggest crowds I ever perform in front of are when I sing before the Welsh Rugby team's matches at the Millennium Stadium in Cardiff and the other big grounds. I am so proud to be their ambassador, because my Welsh heritage means everything to me, it is what makes me who I am. The Welsh people have a great tradition of choral singing and that is how I learnt to sing, and the Welsh landscape and special places continue to inspire me wherever I travel. I return home to Wales as often as I can, and as well as going to Neath I try to visit the lovely coastline of the Gower peninsula. I may live in London now, but home to me will always mean Wales, and Neath in particular.

PHOENIX FROM THE ASHES

BY GEORGE FERGUSON
ACANTHUS FERGUSON MANN ARCHITECTS
AND IMMEDIATE PAST PRESIDENT, RIBA

The story of today's thriving mixed use Tobacco Factory is one of corporate might, planning myopia, and of gentle, progressive private regeneration. In the early 1970s Imperial Tobacco undertook the development of a new HQ and factory at Hartcliffe, a 1960s residential council estate on Bristol's southern boundary. Designed by the Chicago architects SOM, in conjunction with the British practice YRM, the structure was built with a design life of some 800 years but was only to remain in use for barely 15.

The building of the Hartcliffe HQ and factory sounded the death knell for both the great Bristol Imperial sites: just south of the river at East Street, Bedminster and at Raleigh Road, Ashton. These sites had been developed at the turn of the century, bringing together various parts of the Imperial Group, dominated by the great Bristol company of WD & HO Wills with its famous brands. The factories were remarkable in their time and were largely designed by the architect Sir Frank Wills – a leading member of the family and Lord Mayor of Bristol.

What is now known as the Tobacco Factory is just one corner of the Raleigh Road site. The whole site – constituting approximately one million square feet of factory buildings – had been sold on to private developers, apart from one building at its northern end, now occupied as Imperial's HQ. I gave evidence at a planning inquiry against the total demolition and subsequently developed

a sketch plan entitled 'a sustainable urban village'. This was not enough to persuade either Bristol's planners or English Heritage of the merits of the buildings. My faith in the planning and heritage protection system took a further dive.

Not being prepared to contemplate defeat, and failing to find anyone to buy the buildings, I decided to make a silly offer for the corner site on which stood some 40,000 sq ft of robust brick building. To my amazement the receiver accepted my desultory offer equating to £5 per sq ft and I had to scrabble around to raise the money. What I did not realise was how difficult it would be to find an agent/valuer who would give it a greater value than I had paid for it – so I had nothing to offer the bank – and what is more my property agent friends thought I was mad. They were right – but I like to feel that I had the last laugh.

Having bought the building in the middle of a deep property recession in the mid 90's, I knew that I would have to dream up a purpose. I had to watch in agony while the demolition contractors wrecked those other fine buildings – for which I had held such hope – but I salvaged what I could including a pair of great cast iron gates from one of the other factory entrances. My attempt at salvaging the terracotta lions and cherubs over the doorway of Factory no 2 was thwarted by them falling apart on removal.

The adjoining site had been sold to Aldi, and the one next to that to a nursing home operator – both resulting in 'bungalow' developments, which seemed to me a wicked waste standing on the sites of magnificent four and five storey courtyard buildings for which I had had such great plans. I decided that it was an ideal opportunity to demonstrate to my sceptical property agent friends and foes that everything they preached to my clients about the wisdom of single use 'monoculture' development was misguided. I was determined to show them that the more you mixed it the better it would be! The challenge was that I found myself with a building beautifully sited at one end of a run down high street in an area that was suffering from depression at the loss of its staple industry and employer.

Having no money to spend on the building I first let some artists in to occupy space and to protect it from the local villains who were breaking windows, vandalising the interior and stripping the lead flashings from the roof. The artists joined the pigeons, but were never going to be a fixture, however I felt strongly that the Tobacco Factory had to put the arts at its core. My instinct was that this should be the performing arts – and that it should strive to give a new heart to the community and to the 'cultural desert' of South Bristol.

Serendipity would have it that the small but adventurous Show of Strength theatre company, who had moved from the nearby Hen & Chicken pub into the Broadmead shopping centre, had realised the need to be back in a real community and approached me about taking some performance space. It fitted my plans – but not my pocket – so, having identified a space on the first floor that had been part of Imperial's head office and disguised as a standard suspended ceiling office interior, I stripped it bare, back to its concrete 12ft high ceiling, steel columns and timber and quarry tile floor, leaving only a few ducts etc to maintain the factory character, and I left them to paint it black, bolt up some lights, and get on with it. That was the birth of the Tobacco Factory theatre – and I have been intent on building on that rough and ready beginning without losing its rough and ready character that is so appealing – if not a bit hot at times!

Other things had been happening around the building while the story of the theatre unfolded, two of which were very relevant to the theatre. What we soon discovered was that theatres bring with them people who want to eat and drink. It was therefore serendipity again that I heard of Teoh's in St Pauls – an economic oriental restaurant run by a remarkable Malysian businessman. It took little to persuade either of us that this was a good move – and just what I was looking for in terms of a very affordable eatery. The second came in the form of a 'performance school' for young people, who occupied the studios that we had created on the remainder of the first floor. Apart from bringing all the teenage dancing and singing wannabe's to the Factory, they also took over the management of letting the studios for sessions to everything from the splendid Rocktap for kids to martial arts.

"I stripped it bare, back to its concrete 12ft high ceiling, steel columns and timber and quarry tile floor, leaving only a few ducts."

So here we have a community of activity – but that cannot live on oriental food and chips alone. I had travelled the world and I knew the sort of thing that I felt would be appropriate for such a robust ex-industrial building. I had stayed for some time in an artist's loft in downtown Manhattan in 2000 and was particularly impressed by New York's robust metropolitan mix. It was this that I wanted to achieve – somewhere that had urban 'edge' but was not scary to anyone of whatever age or background – and was above all 'affordable'.

I returned with a clear vision for the Tobacco Factory café/bar. I would, as I had done with the rest of the building, strip it back to its basics – and what I added back would reflect its industrial character. Nothing would be hidden behind some ghastly beer stained patterned carpet or softened with curtains or cushions. This was to be an independent and indestructible place with no pretensions. As I did wherever I could in the building, I 'went with the flow' keeping all that was sensible, in this case turning a laboratory cold store, with its impressive doors, into the cellar – putting it at the heart of the operation. This approach makes decisions for you – it is not a cop-out but a fundamental aspect of sustainable conversion, as was the desire to reuse as much in the way of elements and materials as was possible.

To emphasise the cultural link with the Theatre we retained one independent room, the Green Room, now ironically painted red, which has a multi-purpose function as a softer retreat from the rough tough main space, and is hired for a medley of purposes from business to community. It is the venue for 'Think Factory', including the regular Science Café, and now Future Shorts, a monthly short film programme – and many things beside. But the biggest leap was in the reduction of the car park to form outside eating and drinking space in 'The Yard' – giving us the al fresco life that was so necessary to compete with the city centre and its waterfront bars. The real triumph is that it attracts such a breadth of clientele – which is what gives me greatest pleasure and what I regard as the real judgement of what we have done.

Education was always to play its part so it was very appropriate that the Bower Ashton Art College, now part of the University of Western England, should apply to bring its new animation course onto our second floor. This followed their early use of the theatre space for their annual fashion show and party. The rest of the second floor was taken by local computer and creative industry companies.

The seven lofts on the third floor – true Manhattan lofts influenced by my 2000 New York stay, as opposed to the bogus 'loft style' apartments so universally marketed by residential developers – are large spaces varying from over 90 to 200 sq m for which I gained both live and work planning designations to maintain flexibility. They are all totally open plan with the exception of the loo – and a semi-enclosed wet room. They have reclaimed timber floors, industrial fittings and kitchens constructed out of a German steel workshop system. As it happens the majority are currently in work mode with occupants varying from conservators to computer graphics, with only lofts 1 and 2 in residential use, including mine, but the balance will change with demand. Living above the shop has its pleasures and its pains – but the pleasures far outweigh!

I have been determined to put the Tobacco Factory at the centre of the sustainability and energy efficiency debate. It has been at the back of my mind in everything I have done in terms of reuse and sensible use of material. With this in mind we are now looking at all opportunities to reduce demand as well as to develop more efficient and renewable systems. The aim is to move towards carbon neutrality – and to generate as much as we can on site – before offsetting the rest with such things as the planting of trees and investing in off-site generation.

"Living above the shop has its pleasures and its pains – but the pleasures far outweigh!"

Most of all I do not see the Tobacco Factory as a project with an end. It will continue developing throughout my lifetime and hopefully beyond. The theatre will of course develop its programme and audience under the care of the Tobacco Factory Arts Trust and the rest of the building will change to react to circumstances, but with its principal principles remaining intact.

Maybe one of the things that gives me the most wicked satisfaction is to see those property agents, who thought I was mad buying the building in the first place and who were religiously opposed to the sort of extreme mixed use that I have been advocating, bringing their clients in for lunch to show them how it can be done. When they then hire us to do the work, satisfaction turns into a real dividend – at least for the practice which I have built up but reduced my share in to spend some time on these other aspects which are beyond architecture, and yet at the same time very much about bringing the built environment to life.

The postscript to this story is the regeneration of the 1970's Hartcliffe Imperial HQ building, which has been bought by the developers Urban Splash who have commissioned us to convert it into a great new living community in an area that so desperately needs a boost.

REGENERATION **PROJECTS**

BY TONY PIDGLEY
MANAGING DIRECTOR,
THE BERKELEY GROUP

One of the most compelling elements of Britain's diverse heritage is its built environment. Indeed, there are few places in the world with such a rich architectural tradition as Britain. Preserving that heritage for future generations is a national responsibility, and for those of us who work in the regeneration sector, it's one that must be taken very seriously indeed. Despite this, the past was perhaps characterised by a prevalent assumption – misplaced I believe – that construction was fundamentally at odds with conservation; that the outlooks and aims of the housebuilding industry stood in opposition to those who quite rightly wanted to protect that heritage.

That was quite wrong. And today, the false label of "housebuilders as the enemies of tradition" is one that – thankfully – is largely no longer applied. The reinvigoration of so many historic, yet neglected, buildings is now a central feature of urban regeneration in this country. And there are a great many opportunities for that

to flourish: for while this country can be justifiably proud of its built heritage, it must also be acknowledged that there are, unfortunately, a great many neglected and unloved buildings across the country, not least in London and the South East. These are often incredibly important, both architecturally and historically, and yet they are allowed to stagnate, as their glory fades further into the sands of memory. It is surely our duty – developers and public alike – to bring these glorious buildings back to use, so that they can be enjoyed again by all.

Of course, I freely admit to my bias on this issue. But I believe that results speak for themselves. So please allow me to highlight some of Berkeley's most recent and largest projects: The Royal Arsenal in Woolwich, Gunwharf Quays in Portsmouth and Royal Clarence Yard, in Gosport which are but a few examples of the way in which companies like us work, successfully I believe, with historic sites, rather than in spite of them. These prove the absurdity of the notion that conservation cannot sit alongside regeneration; and they show how our industry is more than capable of working with a site's heritage rather than against it. The reinvigoration of historic sites and buildings such as these is brownfield regeneration at its very best and they are the developments of which I am most proud.

Of course, the challenges associated with such sites are huge, and unique. Berkeley and I have certainly learned much as we have progressed; indeed we are still learning. But one thing that we have always known to be of fundamental importance was the priceless benefit of consultation with local and national experts, enabling us to place sites such as Gunwharf in the context that would again bring them to life. I think that what has been key in our own development in this area has been our willingness to work with public bodies and other partners, who have been able to offer their precious insight into how best to approach the unique and local challenges that heritage sites pose.

For instance, at Charter Quay – our development in Kingston-upon-Thames – we worked closely with a number of public bodies and consultation groups to ensure that the design combined contemporary style with the historic market square frontage. This incorporated medieval, Stuart and Georgian features, reflecting the historic urban landscape. We were careful to blend the original features with a modern setting, and restored and incorporated a Jacobean staircase into one of the new shops, providing a tangible physical link between the old Castle Inn, where the original staircase stood, and the new development.

At Charter Quay, Gunwharf, Royal Clarence Yard and many other projects, we have always been careful to show due respect for the buildings we work with and, more importantly, for the artisans and artists who originally crafted them. If approached with the sensitivity and care that they deserve and demand, the reinvigoration of historic buildings can produce the most staggering results and can be a wonderful focal point for wider regeneration schemes. They are, of course, more complex and difficult than many other more 'normal' projects, but this must not serve as a deterrent to regeneration. It should instead be a spur to innovation. It is, I believe, precisely because of this complexity that the ensuing results are so impressive. Meeting the challenges posed by heritage sites has provoked urban regeneration dramatically to improve and to adopt new approaches and techniques. It has also, critically, brought a great many important buildings back to use.

"To go to Portsmouth on a Saturday afternoon and to see the old naval buildings busy and popular is a great source of personal pride and pleasure."

This, for me, is the key. To go to Portsmouth on a Saturday afternoon and to see the old naval buildings busy and popular is a great source of personal pride and pleasure. Buildings such as these should not be allowed to fester, empty and unloved. Putting them to 21st century use, while retaining the character, charms and significance of their past is, I believe, the best and most deserving way in which they can survive another century and preserve their importance for future generations.

If Berkeley is already known for the innovative and attractive contemporary developments that it create, then I would be delighted if we could become equally renowned for our ability to reinvigorate historic buildings, bringing them back to use with the imagination and vigour that they deserve. Respecting the craftsmen and women who built these magnificent structures, and giving authenticity to our new developments by connecting existing and new communities to our heritage. I hope that we are some way towards achieving this. Wherever our developments may be located, our focus is always on the legacy that they leave for the community and for future generations. And so, it is with one eye on the future that we ensure that we have the other on the past.

PREVIOUS PAGE
Gunwharf Quays, Portsmouth

THIS PAGE
Facing page: Bird's eye view of Gunwharf Quays
This page, top: The Royal Arsenal, Woolwich
This page, below: Royal Clarence Yard, Gosport

OVERLEAF
Gunwharf Quays and the Spinnaker Tower, Portsmouth

ROBERT GORDON'S **COLLEGE**

BY MICHAEL GOVE MP
SHADOW MINISTER FOR HOUSING
AND MP FOR SURREY HEATH

We shape buildings, and then they shape us. The buildings which shaped me in my most formative years were all hewn from one rock – granite. As a child of Aberdeen I grew up in a 1930s granite semi, was educated in a series of forbidding granite buildings of Victorian and Georgian vintage, learned to love literature in a magnificent granite public library and worshipped in austere Presbyterian majesty in a series of granite kirks. Granite is an unyielding stone, formed as a result of volcanic pressures which give it a certain robustness. But while its dominant aspect is grey it retains the capacity to surprise. The veins of quartz which run through granite blocks give a curious sparkle to otherwise restrained surfaces, and in the right light can lend playfulness to sober designs.

Why someone brought up in an environment like that should end up as a polemical journalist and then a Conservative MP I leave to better minds than mine. But whatever skills I have which help me in my trade I owe to one particular granite building above all – Robert Gordon's College.

RGC is now a modern, co-educational, independent school in the heart of Aberdeen with all the facilities, from IT connectivity to manicured playing fields, one would expect of a model 21st century educational establishment. But at its heart is a remarkable building, the Auld Hoose, which is the legacy of a remarkable man.

The Robert Gordon who established the modern foundations of the school which bears his name was the son of an advocate and the grandson of another Robert Gordon, of Straloch, the cartographer who put Scotland on the map in Blaeu's atlas of 1654. The younger Robert Gordon was born in 1668, left fatherless at the age of 12, graduated from Aberdeen University at the age of 21 and then embarked on a hugely successful career as a merchant in the Baltic.

Trading with the ports of the Hanseatic League, Gordon was typical of many Scots of his time in making his way abroad. There were thousands of Scots working in Eastern Europe, in the countries which are now Russia, the Baltic States and Poland. And, like many enterprising Scots, before and since, he was a philanthropist. On his death in 1731, he left his entire estate to be used in building a residential school for educating young boys.

Robert Gordon's Hospital, as it was first known, first accepted boys in 1750. The delay in opening the establishment was not due to the sorts of planning issues which so bedevil imaginative new developments today, but for broader reasons of state. The handsome granite building which became the hospital was first occupied by Hanoverian soldiers serving under the Duke of Cumberland, or Butcher Cumberland as he was known, the general charged with putting down the 1745-6 Jacobite rebellion.

Treading the stones of that original building today it is possible to imagine redcoats hurrying up the worn-down stairs to the handsome panelled room where the school governors now meet in order to receive orders from their periwigged officers.

Since 1750 the original foundation laid by Robert Gordon has expanded. The Hospital has become a school with over 1,000 pupils, from the ages of five to 18, which has long outgrown the original Georgian building at its heart. There are now handsome wings, science and PE blocks, a separate junior school, assembly hall and language labs. There is also a junior brother institution, which has long since grown up, Robert Gordon's University, originally an Institute of Technology, which shares some of the school's grounds and which enjoys a world-wide reputation, not least in those skills and sciences related to marine exploration and the oil industry.

But at the heart of the campus still, is the original building which has preserved its fabric and character for the last 250 years. Thinking of it always inspires nostalgia in me, for classrooms with desks from the 1930s, which still sported inkwells, long since dried out, for blackboards on which memorable dates were chalked long before whiteboards carried slide shows, and for the private eyrie at the top of the building which became the prefects' room, a long, low garret, much like the one in which Mimi might have expired in *La Bohème*, but filled with boys consuming mutton pies and iron brew rather than tragically consumptive heroines.

One of the glories of granite, certainly as used in Aberdeen, is the way in which even domestic architecture is lent a certain majesty. Walk through the residential streets of Aberdeen's West End and you'll see handsome family homes with baronial flourishes, the odd crenellation and Gothick touch adding character to otherwise solid bourgeois residences.

The original RGC building, the Auld Hoose, is majestic in a perhaps more restrained fashion. A classic piece of Georgian building, albeit in a material not often associated with the finest work of that period, the Auld Hoose was the work of William Adam, father of the more famous Robert Adam.

Among William Adam's other notable works are Haddo House, the home of the Marchioness of Aberdeen, and Duff House, in Banff, the historic seat of the Earls of Fife and now a museum, run jointly by Aberdeenshire Council, the quango Historic Scotland and The National Galleries of Scotland. I can recommend a visit to both, not least because they are both vibrant centres of artistic endeavour, through the work of the Haddo House Choral and Operatic Society and The Friends of Duff House.

The obvious jumping-off point for either, however, would be a trip to Aberdeen and no visit to Aberdeen would be complete without a tour round Robert Gordon's College. The entrance to the school is guarded by the statue of another famous Gordon, General Charles, the Victorian hero who fell at Khartoum. Gordon is, incidentally, commemorated at another fine school, Gordon's School in West End, near Woking in Surrey, which boasts, like RGC, a pipe band as well as a superb academic record.

The approach to Robert Gordon's College runs past Aberdeen's Art Gallery and the University with the Auld Hoose dominating the vista at the end of the drive. Handsomely proportioned, with an alcove set just above the door for a statue of the founder, the building manages to retain inside as much as possible of its external character. On the first floor, the Governors' Room and Headmaster's offices boast many original features, including the panelling and (now defunct) fireplaces. The iron rule of the health and safety bureaucrats means that, inevitably, some of the building's original charm has been sacrificed to satisfy contemporary pre-occupations but more than enough survives of the building's original spirit to infuse the school with a special character.

The knowledge, while at school, that the superb education we received was due, at root, to the vision and generosity of an individual separated from us by 200 years couldn't help but give us a deeper appreciation of how much our schooling mattered and how very lucky, in historical terms, we were to be in such fortunate circumstances. Robert Gordon's story is a reminder that public goods depend on private enterprise, an engagement with the wider world sits most naturally with a strong affection for one's birthplace, and handsome buildings which lift the spirits can help create successful communities with a sense of purpose. Which is why I'm proud to be one his original foundation's beneficiaries.

"...it is possible to imagine redcoats hurrying up the worn-down stairs to the handsome panelled room where the school governors now meet in order to receive orders from their periwigged officers."

HYDE PARK AND KENSINGTON GARDENS

BY EMILY MAITLIS
BBC *NEWSNIGHT* PRESENTER

If places could have stalkers I'd probably have been arrested by now. Hyde Park has been in my veins for as long as I can remember. Taken there as a child by my father to row (in both senses of the word) on the Serpentine, I now live a stone's throw from it and find an excuse to wander through it, to it or around it about three times a day. You see? Obsessive/compulsive behaviour. There are parts of it I fear I may be banned from altogether. Kensington Palace is the chief one. The lady on the gate now winces when she sees me coming. More accurately, winces when she sees me, accompanied by my two-year-old son heading towards her sanctuary. He is enthralled by the velvet cordons that line the verges, swishing up to the main house – an affection he conveys most energetically by entangling them one by one in his own version of a Mexican wave. He assumes the pebbles that grace the pathways are for hurling, the unfeasibly immaculate grass good enough to eat. And when this thuggish behaviour is about to take hold and I see her steaming galleon-like towards us – with the full force I like to imagine of the WI in her sails – I can only lower my eyes and whisper through my fringe 'I'm sure it's what Diana would have wanted'. Her look tells me it is not.

When we're not inadvertently destroying gems of the monarchy, there is always the Pirate Ship sandpit in the North of the Park. I used to think this was a mere kiddies' playground. How naïve.

More recently I've woken up to the fact this is where all the big deals are made, relationships forged, information traded. I have a suspicion its adventure park is a training ground for all those Alpha males who intend to win the parents' race at their child's sports day. The faces are often familiar there – not so much because they're neighbours or friends – but because you discover (moments too late after that friendly nod of greeting) they turn out to be Paul Weller, Patsy Kensit or the odd Channel 4 presenter. My husband once told me – in the hushed slightly strangled tone one uses when admitting under pressure to a spouse they have put on weight – my running kit (a cake-mix stained sleeveless blue fleece) was not really up to Pirate Ship standards. Embarrassed to say I ditched it soon afterwards for something slithery, black and embossed so I would not be tagged shameful parents as my kids grew older.

Hyde Park though, has seen me at my most carefree and at my most shocking. Rollerblading as a reckless twenty-something student with the world at my feet. Rollerblading as an exhausted thirty-something still pretending to be a reckless student. Power walking a sleepless baby before dawn – my only defence against would-be muggers the ear splitting screams emanating from the papoose (in retrospect I doubt I have ever been safer). Running at eight months pregnant – an act the untrained eye might unkindly interpret as the incontinent shuffle of someone in need of a public convenience. Recalling the lazy summer afternoon a decade earlier where, over bottles of wine, my sisters and I once discussed whether we'd bear each other's children if we couldn't – God forbid – carry our own. The intensity of the thoughts at odds with the serenity of our surroundings and the odd frisbee lobbed into our laps from afar.

The first day my husband and I ever spent together in London was walking down that extraordinary avenue of embassies that lines the park. We were trying to guess each one's country of origin. He, the conventional *Boys Own* way by national flag. Me, the *Good Housekeeping* route of female intuition... Bare Stalinish box, bad curtains? Probably Russian. Gold embossed flowerbeds? Probably an Emirate. Seventeen thousand security guards? Had to be Israeli. We ended our walk at the round pond, that bleak New Year's Day, little imagining that nearly a decade later we would come to know virtually every swan on it by name.

Nowdays, feeding those ducks forms a major part of my work/life balance. When I was growing up in Sheffield, it used to be the odd stale crust flung hopelessly across a muddy stream in their direction. But my son takes this task very seriously indeed. We have to go

and buy bread specifically. And I like to imagine these creatures – products of such a rarified environment – know their gluten free wheat free ciabatta from their organic Sudanese soda bread. Never seen a lactose-intolerant mallard? You haven't had the full Hyde Park experience.

When I first arrived back in London after nearly seven years in the Far East, I remember that sense of being riveted by Speakers' Corner. Having felt exlcuded from the political process and any kind of debate by my lack of vote and failure to learn Cantonese out there, suddenly this talk, this argument was all aimed at ME. I would stand as spellbound by the snappily dressed black guys from the Nation of Islam with their car-salesman patter, as by the bearded wanderer in full length gown embarking on an extraordinary treatise about the demise of capitalism and the oil markets. What struck me was the clash of their fiery passions with the bemused yet disengaged tolerance of the gathered crowds. It was a luxury, I saw for the first time, to have a place where speech was so free it barely had any currency to the listening ears. We came there for entertainment, not liberation. Indeed I remember once clutching the wrist of a uniformed policeman I found there – not to shield me from the force of wild and provocative diatribe,

"We ended our walk at the round pond ... little imagining that nearly a decade later we would come to know virtually every swan on it by name."

but quite simply because I'd cascaded down to the Corner on the flimsiest of aforementioned rollerblades and needed the strong arm of the law in the most literal sense.

That was several years ago now. And I wonder if the events in Iraq, London and certainly new race hate legislation have added a sharper edge to what goes on there today. Either way, it all seems to exemplify what I love about Hyde Park. The – dare I say – organic nature of a place that has seen all faces and heard all things. That plays host to spontaneous capoeira dance on a random Sunday afternoon, or transforms itself into an historic Live8 venue one fateful night in July when promises are made to change the world. A place that has been turned subversive shades of pink by the annual Mardi Gras parade, or traditionally decked in union flags to greet a somewhat more conservatively dressed Queen.

That image of Kensington Gardens awash with wreaths in the September of 1997 will probably never leave me. Column inches may have struggled to understand this 'outpouring of national grief for Diana – so at odds with our national psyche'. But whether people knew for what they were mourning or not, it was the park once again that offered a focus for collective emotion. A skein of which is captured even now by every passing tourist who demands a snapshot of themselves before her palace gates.

At the other end of the spectrum, and indeed the park, that annual event that captures the truest eccentricity of the English – and indeed their optimism. The Remarkable Men in their flying machines who attempt to cross the Serpentine and collapse at the first running jump. Rarely has so little endeavour or expense been spared on such a fruitless task. A task, I now see, that exemplifies so much of what I love about the country in which I live.

I have been to posh summer parties in the Orangery and chaotic family picnics by the pedalos. I have been courted in its secluded pathways and battled with the tantrums of a toddler in its most public arteries. I have been part of a crowd of thousands for its concerts but mostly, I have been alone there. Forget the lungs of London. Hyde Park is my escape from the world.

NEGLECTING OUR PAST

BY SEAN RAFFERTY
BBC RADIO 3 PRESENTER

As I write, the tidal waters of Lough Swilly which once bore the last of the Gaelic chieftains into exile are gently and brightly lapping the shoreline below. In the far distance, atop a hill with breathtaking strategic views of five Irish counties, stands the iron-age fort of Grianan of Aileach, the 9th century home to the northern O'Neills. Swing to the north-west and, on the edge of Inch Island, stands the castle where the O'Donnells once fought over the chieftainship of Tyrconnell. Part of our heritage. Evidence and anchors that link an increasingly disconnected world to a past that made us what we are. Without it, our identity is less rooted – our sense of being part of something greater than the everyday and mundane is diminished.

The tragedy of Irish history has meant that the heritage of story telling, of poetry and of music, of an age when travelling harpists were welcomed in every Great House as honoured guests; the buildings and the landscapes; have all been relegated to Cinderella status. That is now changing! Too late for the wild parts of the west coast, now littered with badly designed and sited dwellings. Too late for many of the great houses, abandoned to ruin and decay, with not much regret. For many of the Big Houses represented an aloof ascendancy, an order imposed. Architecture was not a political priority. And yet, there is now a sadness for what has been lost.

The Gardens of Coole Park, home of Lady Gregory, muse of W.B. Yeats, are now restored and much visited. But the house at its centre is gone.

Bowens Court, the home of the great writer Elizabeth Bowen, was demolished by the farmer who bought it. Essence of 18th century Irish Georgian, it stood square and three storied in its treed demesne. We can only now imagine the author, returning after the war, ingeniously cladding the tall, light-flooded, drawing room windows with the pink corset material she had bought in Soho.

The Palladian ideal manifested itself in Ireland in the great garden – chaste Castle Coole in County Fermanagh, for instance, rising godlike from its park.

It also brought us a generosity of spirit and a sense of proportion to the vernacular: a philosophy we have abandoned, as we cram more and more mean-proportioned houses on to less and less space.

We compensate with theme parks and interpretative centres, which only reduce the real and historic to cuteness. Far better to bring the old into a new world with imagination and respect.

"One day, I hope, there will be a law that will allow me to sue you for disease of spirit. And I'll use it. Not a bad idea actually..."

I grew up on the eastern seaboard of Ireland in County Down. The local big house, Donard Park, had been abandoned, its fine granite bays collapsing, its curvilinear glasshouse against a roaring waterfall smashed and rusting. The walled garden survived – acres of vegetables and soft fruit, and a place of delight and excitement to a small boy on his bicycle sent to buy punnets of strawberries. The smell is with me still, as is the seductive whiff of polish and damp that is part of the ancient patina of many a house where memory and character lodge in the very fabric.

Demolition, what we sometimes please to call improvements, and violent change banish these delicate and important links to the past, and leave us the poorer.

Fanciful? Over romantic? It is a nebulous thing, this heritage, and a precious one. It needs our respect in all its manifestations.

I once met a gentleman developer who, needless to say, lived in a very fine house himself. He had just developed an office block of appalling ugliness and banality next to an exceedingly elegant row of early 18th century houses. An insult, I said. Modern and profitable he said. But I've got to look at this excrescence when I walk up this street, I said, and it pains me.

One day, I hope, there will be a law that will allow me to sue you for disease of spirit. And I'll use it. Not a bad idea actually... What about it?

"Demolition, what we sometimes please to call improvements, and violent change banish these delicate and important links to the past, and leave us the poorer."

PREVIOUS PAGE
Ancient Irish Wall
THIS PAGE
Left: Inch Island from Buncrana
Right: Loch Swilly from the
Grianan Fort, County Donegal
OVERLEAF
Castle Coole

THE OLD VIC

BY SIMON CALLOW
ACTOR, WRITER AND DIRECTOR

The Old Vic always seemed to be somehow part of my life, and my family history – somewhat spuriously, in the latter case, as it now seems to me. In a typically Edwardian association, my maternal grandmother claimed a connection because she and her family had worshipped, in St Agnes' Church in Kennington, at the next pew but one down from Emma Cons and her niece Lilian Baylis, successive directors of the theatre; after the service my grandmother's family would exchange nods and greetings with the Misses Cons and Baylis. That was the entire extent of the familiarity, but for an Edwardian it was significant, and placed us, in my grandmother's eyes at any rate, rather closer to the Vic (as she always called it) than ordinary theatre-goers. My mother and her brother and sister duly attended plays there, feeling rather special (though they were more often to be found at ballet or opera performances at Sadler's Wells, that new theatre with an old name which was a late outcrop of Miss Baylis's missionary passion to spread improving culture to the people). The contact with the Old Vic claimed by my paternal

grandmother was more personal, if less spiritual: she played bridge with Annette Clarke, Lilian Baylis's loyal Box Office manager and later assistant, and this pastime resulted in my father and his brothers receiving free tickets for everything at the Vic.

Clarke was long dead by the time my grandmother started taking me there, in the early 1960s, when the theatre was under the direction of Michael Elliot, later creator of the Royal Exchange Theatre in Manchester. She and I had occasionally been to plays in the West End, but this was a very different experience. For a start, Waterloo was, in those days, a far from salubrious quarter, just as it had been in the 1880s when Emma Cons had transformed the disreputable Old Vic (as the Royal Victoria Theatre was quickly dubbed) into the Royal Victoria Hall and Coffee Tavern. Her plan was to lure the locals out of the pubs and gin palaces and into the warm, clean and alcohol-free auditorium, where they would be diverted and improved by classical concerts and the

occasional scene from Shakespeare; little by little, under Lilian Baylis's direction, this evolved into performances of operas and the first full cycle of Shakespeare's plays, and in the 1920s and 30s, still underpinned by Evangelical inspiration and desperately under-funded, it had become the great breeding ground of English classical actors. By 1962, when I started going there, it was as chronically short of money as ever, and the evangelical fervour was flagging. Waterloo itself was of course dominated by the station, at the back end of which the theatre was to be found, a far cry from the ultra-modern glamour of the Royal Festival Hall on the South Bank, with its fine position on the river and its commanding view of the West End, which, though just a bridge away, inhabited another world entirely. The Vic was a somewhat unprepossessing four-square building, part of a block which included a large branch of the grocer David Greig. The effects of bombing were still apparent and the impression was functional rather than glamorous. The Lower Marsh, just behind the station, was a busy market, selling clothes

of golden light. To enter it was to be inducted into another world, halfway between waking and dreaming, one in which something momentous seemed about to happen. Sometimes, bravely, I took myself to see plays there alone, which meant going to the gallery, to the gods, as I quickly learned to call them. One entered by a side entrance, struggled up what seemed like hundreds of stairs and found oneself sitting on wooden benches, clinging vertiginously onto the metal railings. From this position the auditorium seemed even more dramatic, incorporating as it did a view of the rest of the audience, on whom one looked down, rather, well, god-like. Emanating from the Gallery Bar, an aroma of coffee (a direct legacy of Miss Cons, perhaps) permanently pervaded the air. And then suddenly the fanfares would sound – it was generally Shakespeare – and one was immediately in the midst of dynastic struggles, or fearing for star-cross'd lovers or chilled by the dank mists enshrouding some Scottish castle. The coffee pervaded everything.

The productions which so enthralled me were, I realise in retrospect, for the most part serviceable rather than inspired. The days of the Old Vic Company under Elliot were numbered: it had already been announced that the newly-created National Theatre under the direction of Laurence Olivier would be taking up residence in the building. And when, in short order, they did, they brought with them – to say nothing of the greatest actor in the world, a superb ensemble and a clutch of challenging directors – a team of brilliant theatre managers, architects and press officers (many from Sadler's Wells) who radically altered the experience of seeing a play at the Old Vic. The exterior of the theatre hardly changed, though the stage door was switched from the left of the theatre to the right, but internally everything was transformed, from the arrangement of the foyer, which now contained a bookstall and a wide-open box office which radically broke from the tradition of the enclosed, latticed lair of the typical West End theatre, to the graphics announcing the exits and the whereabouts of the bars (very modern), to the colour of the seats (blue) and their arrangement – there was now a gap at row O – and then, most significantly, to the proscenium, which Sean Kenny, Olivier's first designer, reshaped, thrusting the stage forward and eliminating the stage boxes, which were faced with grey boards. The splendour

and household goods rather than food; to the left of the theatre as you entered was The Cut, a run-down suburban street of butchers, greengrocers, pubs and cafés. Directly opposite the theatre was a little green on which were to be found the successors of Miss Cons's original target audience, the so-called winos, though methylated spirits was their more likely tipple, with an occasional Brasso chaser.

One was nipped pretty smartly past these ladies and gents and into the foyer. This was no vision of loveliness, no prelude to romance: plain, practical, unembellished, it was simply the doorway to the auditorium, the general impression of which was dim, the burgundy seats further darkened by the sweat of thousands of backs and buttocks, the gold paint on the balconies and boxes dulled and peeling, the curtain moth-eaten and sagging. Inexplicably, this tattered and tired interior had a thrilling effect: redolent of past excitements, it was utterly unlike the outside world, archaic and mysterious, full of shadows and stray shafts

of the old proscenium arch (however dimmed with age) was now replaced with something functional, even ugly, and the auditorium accordingly lost some of its mystery and charm. The gain was obvious, however, the moment the curtain went up. After the solid and sensible productions of the last days of the Old Vic Company, Olivier and his cohorts offered a riot of colour, in costume, set and performances: sensuality and glamour had returned to the theatre, made all the more dazzling because of the new austerity of the auditorium.

The old place was transformed, and my first visits there, with my school on a typical ILEA matinee outing, instantly revised my understanding of what was possible in the theatre. The acting company was a crack unit, strong at every level, with the old warrior, Olivier, leading from the front; but everybody there – ushers, bookstall staff, coffee vendors, all in their smartly functional uniforms – seemed part of the enterprise, which had a swaggering sense of itself that stemmed directly from the boss. So much so that when I left school, bewildered as to what I should do with my life, I wrote to Olivier, who, by return of post, offered me

"The old place was transformed, and my first visits there, with my school on a typical ILEA matinee outing, instantly revised my understanding of what was possible in the theatre."

a job in the box office, and I then got to know the hidden parts of the building, the many changes Olivier had wrought: the office where we dealt with the mail had been Lilian Baylis's, an electrics store just below ground level had been converted into a canteen, where the whole company, actors, stage hands, box office staff, ate together; staircases had been concealed from the public to accommodate some of the huge administrative staff. Some fairly brutal alterations had been made to the original scheme of the foyers, the walls covered with brown Hessian which could be covering hardboard as likely as bricks. Olivier, he claimed, had never liked the Old Vic, where he had his first classical triumphs, and he certainly transformed the old place. But it remained recognisably Lilian Baylis's theatre. When, later, I became an usher, I discovered that the password in case of fire was "Miss Baylis is in the house", which struck me as rather risky, since many of her original customers were still regular visitors to the

National: they might easily have imagined her wheeling lopsidedly round the corner, frying pan in hand, to take up her usual position in the stage box, there to cook her supper, as was her nightly wont, and had a heart attack.

The spirit of Miss Baylis, in every sense, was finally banished in 1983, when the theatre was magnificently restored, thanks to the selfless generosity of the Canadian magnates, Ed and David Mirvish, The National had left for the South Bank in 1976, and the theatre struggled on, penniless again and without a clear identity; finally the Mirvishes boldly decided to turn the clock back to the days before Miss Cons and her mission, to its second incarnation, as the Royal Victoria Theatre, opened in 1833. An almost new theatre was finally unveiled with a fine portico, flambeaux blazing above it, a splendidly restored foyer, the staircases opened up for public use, the auditorium blindingly red and gold in all its early-Victorian splendour, boxes re-opened, the stage discreetly withdrawn to behind the proscenium arch, which, newly endored, was now crowned with patriotic motifs of the correct period. In the process of refurbishment, the theatre's many palimpsests, the last of which were the mystery-filled dilapidation of Michael Elliot's theatre, and the bracing functionalism of Olivier's, both of which in their different ways expressed Lilian Baylis's ideal of a People's Theatre, and both of which served above all to usher the audience into the presence of the play, had been erased, and a theatre which drew attention to itself and to its audience, had taken its place. It is, on its own terms, a fine playhouse, and an embellishment to a newly chic Cut. Theatres, though, are, in their essences, more than simply buildings and interior decoration: they are an accumulation of the ghosts of endeavours past. At the Old Vic, they seem to have been expunged. The sweat has been expunged from the walls; all the dead dreams dispelled. The winos are still there, though, which is a curious sort of a comfort.

CONCLUSION

When we first thought of producing a book to mark the 30th Anniversary of The Architectural Heritage Fund we wanted to find a way to demonstrate the widespread passion that we know exists for the UK's heritage. Thus came about the idea of asking people who were well-known in their own fields, but not generally associated with heritage issues, to write about their own particular interests and enthusiasms. The results have exceeded our expectations in every way, and have, I hope, proved the case – wherever you look in this rich country, there are buildings and landscapes which are of tremendous significance to people locally and nationally.

At the AHF we support local groups in rescuing buildings and, crucially, in finding a viable use which will give them a new lease of life. In a time of global concern about the environment and our exploitation of it, there can be nothing more genuinely sustainable than the restoration and re-use of a derelict or abandoned building, bringing life to a community and ensuring that the legacy we leave for future generations is a positive one. *Sites Insight* shows how much our heritage and environment means to 12 very different people, and this is echoed throughout the UK across all social and ethnic groups. Only by caring for and regenerating our historic environment can we properly reflect this passion and enthusiasm, and the work of the AHF is geared entirely to helping people to do this.

My final task in writing this conclusion is to thank people, starting with our 12 contributors, all of whom gave their time and enthusiasm to this project with great generosity. Our Trustee, author and World Monuments' Fund Director Colin Amery has edited the book with great skill and has brought his unparalleled knowledge of the UK's heritage and its management to it. Another Trustee, Fionnuala Jay O'Boyle, was instrumental in securing the contributions of several of the authors, and was also an invaluable sounding board throughout. All of my colleagues have supported the project and helped with ideas and advice, and I would like to thank Victor Rose for the picture research, and in particular Diane Kendal, who has managed the production process with her usual unflappable calm, with some helpful advice along the way from my brother, Peter Lush, of London League Publications. Earlier in this book we have acknowledged our sponsors and supporters, and I would finally like to thank Martin Premm-Jones and Neil Fox at our designers, Premm Design, for bringing the words to such splendid visual life, and Steve Hollamby, at Chandlers Printers, for securing a great deal on the paper and producing yet another high quality publication for the AHF.

Ian Lush
Chief Executive
The Architectural Heritage Fund, October 2006